# THE FRENCH THEY NEVER TAUGHT YOU

## Tips for Teachers and Advanced Students

*J.J. Binamé*
*P.G. Socken*

CANADIAN SCHOLARS' PRESS INC.

The French They Never Taught You: Tips for Teachers and Advanced
Students
J. J. Binamé and P. G. Socken

First published in 2002 by
**Canadian Scholars' Press Inc.**
180 Bloor Street West, Suite 1202
Toronto, Ontario
M5S 2V6

www.cspi.org

CSPI gratefully acknowledges the financial support of the Government of
Canada through the Book Publishing Industry Development Program for our
publishing activities.

**National Library of Canada Cataloguing in Publication Data**

Socken, Paul, 1945-
        The French they never taught you : tips for teachers and
advanced students

ISBN 1-55130-214-4

        1. French language--Textbooks for second language learners--English
speakers. 2. French language--Grammar. 3. French language--Vocabulary. 4.
French language--Study and teaching (Higher)--English speakers. I. Binamé,
José, 1915-2001. II. Title.

PC2105.S62 2002            448.2'421            C2002-900406-3

Page layout: Elle Sheldrick
Cover design: George Kirkpatrick

  02   03   04   05   06   07        7   6   5   4   3   2   1

Printed and bound in Canada by Mothersill Printing Inc.

# TABLE OF CONTENTS

## PART TWO: VOCABULARY

# The French They Never Taught You

*Tips for teachers and advanced students*

---

## Preface

What the world does not need now is yet another grammar book outlining the conjugation and use of the present tense in French. We have more than enough books on the French language for beginners. What *is* sorely needed is a manual explaining advanced or nuanced points of vocabulary and grammar either badly explained in existing texts or left entirely unexplored.

With the advent of linguistics, the academic world has been fortunate enough to enjoy the work of sociolinguists, psycholinguists, historical linguists and others, but where is the old-fashioned grammarian who will tell the beleaguered speaker of English, struggling to learn French, the difference between *mots* and *paroles*? They're both just *words* in English.

The following is a simple, down-to-earth language book, designed for the teacher and advanced student of French who already know about the possessive pronoun and for whom the conditional tense holds no mysteries. It is intended for the student who has had revealed to him or her the difference between the *passé composé* and *imparfait* and still can't get it right after doing thirty-eight exercises on the subject. It is intended for the teacher whose students have asked him or her the difference between *nourriture, aliments, denrées alimentaires* and *cuisine* and has had to "cook up" an answer that's unappetizing to both.

There are two major kinds of problems addressed in this manual. One concerns the use of words, lexical questions, such as the difference between *mots* and *paroles*, and the different ways to say *food* in French. The second kind of problem concerns grammar points that may be inadequately explained elsewhere (*passé composé* vs. *imparfait* and agreement of the past participle of pronominal verbs), or that are not explored at all (causal conjunctions: *parce que, car, comme, puisque*, etc.).

Because this compendium is for the teacher and advanced students, it is primarily a reference work and, as such, has few exercises. Exercises are included only when the point at issue is so complex — or has been revealed here for the first time — that we have judged that even the advanced student or teacher would appreciate an opportunity to try his or her hand at its practical application.

My co-author, José Binamé, passed away in the year 2000 and this volume is dedicated in his memory. He was my friend and mentor. When I arrived at the University of Waterloo in 1973, I first met this friendly curmudgeon and I discovered two things: first, he knew more about the French language than anyone I had ever met, and second, that I had a great instinctive feeling of friendship for him.

As the years wore on and we discussed many points of French language, our friendship grew and I set about putting our thoughts on paper to share with others as I had done with my own students. This work is clearly not a work of scholarship but one of many years' experience in the language classroom. It does not claim to be exhaustive. There are other books on difficulties in European French and Canadian French weightier and much more comprehensive, but nothing this focused and with this content.

Criticism can be leveled at what José used to call our "syllabus": It is too "purist" in tone; it is prescriptive rather than descriptive; it is too focused on Canadian usage. I make no apologies for the above. José Binamé was a Belgian of an earlier generation — he died in his eighties — who spent most of his career in Canada and some of his pronouncements and explanations did, indeed, reflect a stricter linguistic world view. Rather than a negative, I see that as liberatingly positive. Today's approach to language and language learning has become so descriptive and unrestricted that I find this method a useful benchmark against which one can measure today's usage. By all means, please feel free to disagree and reject some of the points you see here, but if it has stimulated your thinking about the French language, then we will have succeeded. Please e-mail your comments and suggestions to psocken@watarts.uwaterloo.ca.

Paul Socken

# Part One

# GRAMMAR

# 1. PREPOSITIONS

## A) For — expressing time

i. I have been teaching **for** thirteen years.

When **for** accompanies an English present perfect or past perfect (have been) to express an action that began in the past and continues into the present, French uses *depuis* and the present tense:

*J'enseigne depuis treize ans.*
I have been teaching (and I still am) for thirteen years.

**Note:** I had been teaching for thirteen years when I retired.
*J'enseignais depuis treize ans quand j'ai pris la retraite.*

The use of the negative in the past alters the tenses:

I had not seen him for three years when he died.
*Je ne l'avais pas revu depuis 3 ans quand il est mort.*

ii. When **for** expresses the duration of the action of the verb, French uses *pendant*.

I worked in Toronto **for** three years.
*J'ai travaillé à Toronto **pendant** trois ans.*

Did you work for a period of three years?
Yes, I did.

The action of the verb *working* lasted the whole period of time reported, three years.

3

iii. When **for** does not express the duration of the action of the verb, French uses **pour**.

> I'm going to Montreal for three days.
> *Je vais à Montréal **pour** trois jours.*

The action of the verb, *going to Montreal*, does not last three days. *For* does express duration, but it is the duration of the *stay* resulting from the action of the verb *going*, not the duration of the action itself. *Pour* is often used with verbs meaning *to go*, and also with *être*.

> *Nous avons tout le temps: je suis ici pour au moins un an.*

**Note:** Verbs that inherently express duration (*durer, rester,* etc.) do not normally take a preposition.

> *La beuverie a duré trois jours sans interruption.*
> *Il est resté deux mois à la campagne.*

However, some of these verbs can also be used in particular instances with a preposition expressing duration (*pendant, durant*). This expression of duration often changes position.

> *Il est resté à la campagne pendant deux mois.*
> *Je n'ai dormi que trois heures.*
> *Elle avait attendu au moins un quart d'heure.*

◻ EXERCISE:

Use *pour* or *pendant* to translate FOR in the following sentences:

a. *Je flânerai à Paris **for** trois semaines.*

b. *Marie ira à Paris* **for** *un mois.*

c. *Jacques viendra* **for** *quelques semaines.*

d. *Hélène doit travailler* **for** *cinq heures.*

e. *Je parlerai* **for** *une heure.*

f. *Pierre s'est promené* **for** *une heure.*

g. *Ils marcheront* **for** *trois quarts d'heure.*

h. *Il a plu* **for** *deux heures.*

i. *Denise sortira* **for** *une demi-heure.*

j. *Nous jouons généralement* **for** *trois heures.*

k. *Les élèves peuvent poser des questions* **for** *vingt minutes.*

KEY:

| | | |
|---|---|---|
| a. *pendant* | b. *pour* | c. *pour* |
| d. *pendant* | e. *pendant* | f. *pendant* |
| g. *pendant* | h. *pendant* | i. *pour* |
| j. *pendant* | k. *pendant* | |

---

## B) To + infinitive

i. **To + Infinitive** is translated by *pour*

a) when the infinitive is preceded by *too*:

He is **too** old to run.
*Il est **trop** vieux **pour** courir.*

b) when *to* means *in order to*:

I did it **to** help you.
*Je l'ai fait **pour** vous aider.*

5

ii. **To + Infinitive** is translated by *de*, *à*, or by no preposition in all other cases:

    a) after an adjective:

        ***facile à*** *faire*
        ***heureux de*** *vivre*

**But**: *Il est facile **de** commettre des erreurs.*

    b) after a verb:

        *autoriser à*
        *interdire de*
        *aller*

**Note:** Whether *à*, *de*, or no preposition is used is often a question of vocabulary, not of grammar.

To determine the correct preposition, refer to a textbook under the chapter titles "Prepositions" or "Infinitive," or consult a dictionary.

## 2) ADVERBIAL PHRASES

---

*Adverbial phrases of place*

How do you say *a knock at the door* in French? If you said *un coup à la porte*, you need to study the following very carefully.

In English, an adverbial phrase of place is often used to modify a noun:

    The man **in** *the street*

In French, this construction is not normally used. An adverbial phrase of place modifies a verb.

*Translation Problems:*

The adverbial phrase of place *can* be used to modify a noun in certain cases established by usage.

> *Son retour* **parmi** *nous.*
>
> *Un coup* **en dessous** *de la ceinture.*
>
> *une villa* **au bord de** *la mer.*

Certain set expressions use the preposition *de*:

> *L'homme* **de** *la rue*
>
> *Tous les livres* **de** *ma bibliothèque*

In most cases, however, where English uses an adverbial phrase of place to modify a noun, French inserts a verb that does not appear in the English:

> The books **on** *my shelves.*
> *Les livres* **qui se trouvent** *sur les rayons de ma bibliothèque.*

> The papers **in** *my briefcase.*
> *Les papiers* **que j'ai** *dans ma serviette.*

◻ EXERCISE:

Translate the following:

　　a. A knock at the door.

　　b. The horse in the corral, there.

　　c. The sandy area between the beach and the road.

　　d. The difference in our points of view.

　　e. A novel by Gabrielle Roy.

　　f. The flowers in the sitting room (salon).

　　g. The documents in my briefcase.

KEY:

a. Un coup *frappé* à la porte.

b. Le cheval *qui trotte* (or qui galope or qui broute, etc.) là-bas dans l'enclos.

c. Le terrain sablonneux *qui sépare* la plage de la route.

d. La différence *qui sépare* nos points de vue. (Adverbial phrase is acceptable here: *la différence entre nos points de vue.*)

e. Un roman *de* Gabrielle Roy.

f. Les fleurs *qui* parfumaient (or qui ornaient, qui égayaient, etc.) le salon.

g. Les documents *que j'ai* dans ma serviette.

## 3) PRONOUNS

---

### A) *Dont or duquel?*

   i. In French, the preposition *de* followed by a relative pronoun (*de qui, duquel,* etc.) **must** be replaced by dont:

     *Voilà justement l'étudiante* **dont** *je te parlais tout à l'heure.*

   ii. However, if the preposition *de* is part of a prepositional phrase, *dont* cannot be used:

     *L'arbre* **au pied duquel** *je m'étais assis...*

     Examples of prepositional phrases: *à partir de, au moyen de, auprès de, autour de, près de, à cause de, en souvenir de,* etc.

## B) On ... Vous

**On** est content si quelqu'un **vous** fait un compliment.

**On** is the normal form of the indefinite pronoun subject. Its object form is **vous**.

**Note:** The possessive adjective representing **on** is **son** (**sa, ses**):

*On est généralement mécontent de son sort.*

But the possessive adjective representing **vous** is **votre**:

*On est content si quelqu'un vous fait un compliment sur votre élégance.*

**Comment:** The above construction is normally avoided:

*On est heureux de recevoir des compliments.*

*Rien ne plaît comme un compliment, surtout s'il est mérité.*

## 4) VERBS

### A) Agreement of the past participle of pronominal verbs

When the pronoun is neither a direct object nor an indirect object; that is, when the pronoun has no logical function, the past participle agrees with the subject.

In all other cases, the past participle agrees as if it were conjugated with the auxiliary *avoir*: the past participle agrees with a preceding DIRECT object.

> *Elle s'est coupée au doigt.* (se is a direct object; past participle agrees with preceding direct object)

*Pierre et Paul se sont battus.* (*se* is a direct object)

*Elle s'est* **coupé** *le doigt.* (*se* is an indirect object; no agreement)

*Pierre et Paul se sont dit des injures.* (*se* is an indirect object; no agreement).

In the following examples, *se* has no logical function. The past participle agrees with the subject.

*Elles se sont aperçues de leur erreur.*

*Elle se sont évanouies.*

*Ils se sont enfuis.*

**Exceptions:** *S'imaginer, se plaire, se complaire, se déplaire, se rendre compte* and *se rire.* (No agreement.)

*Nous ne nous étions pas imaginé que Luc et Laura s'étaient plu au premier coup d'œil: nous ne nous étions rendu compte de rien.*

---

B) *Plus-que-parfait or passé antérieur (passé surcomposé)?*

i. When English uses a pluperfect (I had done), French uses the *plus-que-parfait* (*j'avais fait*), except in the following case:

ii. After a conjunction of time, verbs not representing an habitual action are put in the *passé antérieur* (*j'eus fait*: written French) or in the *passé surcomposé* (*j'ai eu fait*: spoken French).

When he had finished his lunch, he smoked his pipe.
*Lorsqu'il eut fini de déjeuner, il fuma une pipe.*

**Note:** The *passé surcomposé* is the oral form of the *passé antérieur*:

> *Lorsqu'il a eu fini de déjeuner, il a fumé une pipe.*

(One can also say *Après avoir déjeuné* or *après son déjeuner* and avoid the construction altogether.)

The *passé antérieur* is used in written French, but the *passé surcomposé* is not normally used, as it is awkward.

Compare with a habitual action: *Lorsque (= chaque fois que) il avait fini de déjeuner, il fumait une pipe.*

---

## C) *Je l'ai vue les voler*

The past participle used with the auxiliary *avoir* and followed by an infinitive agrees with the preceding pronoun object **if that pronoun causes the action of the infinitive.**

In the example above, she stole something (I saw her steal them).

> *Les chansons que j'ai entendu chanter...*
>
> *Les jeunes filles que j'ai entendues chanter...*

In the first example, the songs are not singing. They are not causing or doing the action of the infinitive, and so there is no agreement.

In the second example, the girls are singing, and so there is agreement.

**Note:** 1. In the faire causative construction, *fait* never agrees because it never causes the action of the infinitive.

2. For *laisser*, usage varies.

> *Elle ne s'est pas fait prier.*
> *Elle ne s'est pas laissée aller.*
> or *Elle ne s'est pas laissé aller.*

---

## D) The passive versus the active voice

Pronominal verbs are used to express the passive voice only when the meaning is generalized:

> *Les livres se sont bien vendus.*

Specific cases are rendered by the passive voice:

> *Un exemplaire de ton livre a été vendu hier.*

---

## E) Imparfait, passé simple and passé composé: the traditional approach

I.  The *passé simple* is the most frequently used tense in literary French: it expresses narrative time.

In general, when telling a story in writing, one has a choice between the *imparfait* and the *passé simple* when English uses the simple past (or preterit).

The *passé simple* has disappeared from spoken French, where the *passé composé* has replaced it. In spoken French, therefore, the choice is between the *imparfait* and the *passé composé* when English uses the simple past.

The *imparfait* is used

i.   When the English uses a form of *was doing* or *used to do*

ii.  When one is describing a situation such as it existed at a given moment (how things were at that time).

*C'était un homme jeune encore qui portait
les cheveux courts.*

The *passé simple* (for the written language) or the *passé
composé* (for the spoken language) is used:

i.  When the verb is accompanied by one of the following
    temporal signs:

    a. the beginning of an action

    *J'ai vécu en Europe **à partir de 1960**. Il arri-
    va à **midi**.*

    b. the end of an action

    *J'y travaillai (ou j'y ai travaillé) **jusqu'en
    décembre**.*

    c. the beginning and end of an action

    *Je séjournai (ou j'ai séjourné) dans l'île **du
    3 au 24 novembre**.*

    d. the length of time of the action (la durée)

    *Je suis resté là **trois ans**. Elle vécut **dix
    ans** en France.*

ii. When one narrates something that happened:

    *Il sauta à cheval et partit à toute allure.*

**Note:** In most cases, the following question helps to decide on
the appropriate tense: Is one describing a situation (how
things were) or is one narrating something that happened?

II. Imparfait

    i.  *Nous **allions** tous les jours manger au restaurant.*

13

Habitual action: customary or usual action in the past

ii. *J'écrivais à ma soeur lorsqu'il entra.*

An action developing in the past, during which a sudden activity occurred.

iii. *Il était fort comme un Turc.*

A description or a state, and not an activity.

iv. Direct Speech: *Elle m'a dit: " Je pars ce soir ".*
Indirect Speech: *Elle m'a dit qu'elle partait ce soir-là.*

v. *Comme j'arrivais, le train partait.*

*Comme* expressing time (in English *as*), takes two imperfects (two activities occurring at the same time).

III. *Passé Simple* (Used in literary French only)

i. *Il entra.*

ii. *Il frappa à coups redoublés.*

(i) and (ii): an action that can be localized or confined in time is presented as having happened once or a number of times in the past.

---

F) *Passé simple (passé composé)/imparfait: a new approach*

The single most difficult aspect of the French language for English speakers is the distinction between the *passé simple* (or *passé composé*) and the *imparfait*.

Even the best English speakers of French occasionally—
*pour ne pas dire plus*—choose the wrong tense.

Following, you will find a helpful approach to the problem,
one that will require concentration and an open mind, but
that will repay your efforts with a new insight. You will be
afforded the opportunity to study the principle, to see some
examples and, finally, to test yourself.

\* \* \*

Since the beginning of recorded time, history can be seen
as a series of actions on a chronological ladder. To isolate
or identify an action on this ladder, the *passé simple* (or
*passé composé*)—the historical tense—is used:

*Victor Hugo naquit en 1802.*

*Jean-Paul arriva au Canada en 1965.*

*Il y vécut trente ans.*

*Je connais très bien Monsieur Bonasse: il a
été mon professeur.*

Now, let us apply the above principle to an analogy. Life is
a film that takes place in the *passé simple*. One can stop
the film at will, in order to describe or explain, in the *imparfait*, a scene, character, situation, state of mind. The *passé
simple* is dynamic and active; the *imparfait* is static and
suited to states of being. The *passé simple* tends to recount
what takes place, is narrative in nature, whereas the *imparfait* recounts how things are and is descriptive in nature:

*Abraham tondait* (description of the setting of our film) *ses
moutons. Sarah vint* (Lights! Camera! Action!) *le rejoindre
et lui dit* (second action) *qu'il fallait* (stop the action! Sarah
must explain the situation) *renvoyer sa deuxième femme
Hagar.*

Let's continue our film analogy with the following example:

I had (1) an interesting discussion with Charles about a tricky point of French grammar.

I wanted (2) to put the past participle in the plural and he maintained (3) that we had to use (4) the singular. We researched (5) it and I was (6) right.

*J'ai eu (1) une discussion intéressante avec Charles sur un point difficile de grammaire française. Je voulais (2) mettre le participe passé au pluriel et il prétendait (3) que nous devions (4) employer le singulier. Nous avons fait (5) des recherches et j'avais (6) raison.*

(1) Lights! Camera! Action! In our film, this is part of the narrative, the first action in a chain of events.

(2), (3) & (4)   Stop the action! I'm giving you some background information on the nature of the event. Answers the question: What was the discussion about? I'm explaining the situation.

(5) Lights, camera, Action! **Second action in the chain of events**. We're back in the narrative mode. This is what we did next. The action is advanced.

(6) Stop the action! No new event took place. I'm explaining the situation.

The following is another example of our theory at work:

I heard (1) my father was flying (2) to Halifax by the next plane. Hoping that he would still be at the airport, I jumped (3) into a taxi, but

a) I arrived (4) too late.
b) when I arrived (5) it was (6) too late.
c) when I arrived (7), I realized (8) it was (9) too late.

*J'ai appris (1) que mon père prenait (2) le prochain avion pour Halifax. Espérant qu'il serait toujours à l'aéroport, j'ai sauté (3) dans un taxi, mais*

a) *je suis arrivé (4) trop tard.*
b) *quand je suis arrivé (5), il était (6) trop tard.*
c) *quand je suis arrivé (7), je me suis rendu compte (8) qu'il était (9) trop tard.*

(1) Lights! Camera! Action! The initial action takes place.
(2) Stop the action! I'm explaining the situation.
(3) This is what happened next. Second action in the chain of events.
(4) This is the next action in the chain; narrates what happened next.
(5) See no. (4).
(6) Describes the situation at the moment of arrival. It is not something that happened next, but rather something that was.
(7) See no. (4).
(8) The action is advanced. I arrived and then I realized. It is what happened next in the chain of events.
(9) *Il était* has the same relationship to *je me suis rendu compte* as *mon père prenait* has to *j'ai appris*: it clarifies the action. In other words, it is not something that happened next, but rather an explanation of the situation at the moment of arrival.

❐ EXERCISE:

Now, try your hand at the following passage to see if you have mastered the concept:

*La porte du restaurant* _____ *1 (être) grande ouverte sur la rue; les murs noircis de fumée* _____ *2 (s'offrir) au regard; des toiles*

d'araignée, dans les coins, _____ 3 (pendre);
l'endroit _____ 4 (paraître) vide, vide et triste.
Lorsque Emmanuel _____ 5 (entrer), il
_____ 6 (apercevoir) Alphonse, immobile, à sa
place habituelle, contre le poêle sans feu. Le jeune homme
allongé sur deux chaises _____ 7 (supporter)
sa tête de ses deux bras croisés sous la nuque et son regard
fixe _____ 8 (paraître) arrêté depuis des heures
sur un point indéchiffrable. Une ombre _____ 9
(s'étendre) sur son visage. Emmanuel _____ 10
(avancer) le bras sur le dossier de la chaise et
_____ 11 (peser) légèrement sur l'épaule
d'Alphonse: 'Eh bien, bonjour, toi.' _____ 12
(dire) -il. Ses yeux _____ 13 (faire) le tour de la
petite salle et _____ 14 (s'arrêter) sur la tenture
qui _____ 15 (masquer) l'arrière-boutique. Il
_____ 16 (prêter) l'oreille et
_____ 17 (entendre) la mère Philibert traîner
ses savates. Vers onze heures, elle _____ 18
(préparer) le repas de son mari qui _____ 19
(revenir) de l'usine à minuit. Un chou qui _____
20 (bouillotter) doucement dans la cuisine
_____ 21 (emplir) le restaurant de son odeur.

Adapted from Gabrielle Roy, *Bonheur d'occasion*


KEY:

1. *était*: description of the setting

2. *s'offraient*: description of the setting

3. *pendaient*: description of the setting

4. *paraissait*: description of the setting

5. *entra*: Lights! Camera! Action! First action in the chain of
   events.

6. *aperçut*: second action in the chain of events.

7. *supportait*: Stop the action! The author is describing a character.

8. *paraissait*: Stop the action! The author is describing a character.

9. *s'étendait*: Stop the action! The author is describing a character.

10. *avança*: Lights! Camera! Action! Third action in the chain.

11. *pesa*: fourth action in the chain of events

12. *dit*: fifth action in the chain

13. *firent*: sixth action

14. *s'arrêtèrent*: seventh action

15. *masquait*: Stop the action! Description of the setting.

16. *prêta*: Action! Eighth action in the chain. This is what happened next.

17. *entendit*: ninth action in the chain. This is what happened next.

18. *préparait*: Stop the action! The author is explaining the situation, describing what la mère Philibert did every night.

19. *revenait*: The author is explaining the situation, describing what the husband did at midnight every night.

20. *bouillottait*: The author is describing the setting.

21. *emplissait*: The author is describing the setting.

**Note:** In **written** French, both *passé simple* and *passé composé* are possible. The *passé simple* is used when there is no connection or link with the present. The *passé composé* can be used to establish a link, direct or indirect, with the present *(Je connais très bien Monsieur Bonasse: il a été mon professeur)*.

## G) *Some basic points about sentence structure*

On the level of meaning, there are two kinds of clauses:

Those that express a state *(Mon chien est petit, Je m'appelle Martine.)*

and

those that express an action *(Je mange un bonbon.)*

**Caution:** Do not take the word *action* literally: *faire, danser, aimer, croire* are actions.

i.   Clauses expressing a state (with verbs *être, paraître, sembler, devenir...*)

There is someone or something (a person, an animal, a thing or an idea) that is in this state: this is the subject.

subject group
*Mon chien est petit.*
subject predicate

The state is qualified by a predicate or subjective completion (*attribut* in French) that ascribes a quality to the subject.

The predicate is linked to the subject by the verb *être*, or a similar verb (*paraître, sembler*, etc.).

ii.  Clauses expressing an action

*Paul a remis la lettre à ton frère cet après-midi.*

subject/verb/          indirect object
direct object          adverbial phrase of time

The action is expressed by the verb.

The one doing the action is the subject.

Who gave the letter to your brother?

The one who undergoes the action is the direct object (Paul gave what to your brother?).

The one who benefits from the action is the indirect object (Paul gave the letter *to whom*?).

The circumstances surrounding the action are expressed by adverbial clauses of:

a) place
b) time
c) cause
d) manner

a)  answer the question where?
b)  answer the questions when? for how long? since when? etc.
c)  answer the question why?
d)  answer the question how?

**Comment:** Direct objects do not have prepositions, indirect objects do.

Indirect objects:

Indirect objects, as mentioned above, usually indicate the beneficiary of the action, but an indirect object can also follow certain combinations of verb + preposition.

e.g.: *parler de, protéger de or contre, se rapporter à*

*Je parle de toi dans ma lettre.*
*parler de quelqu'un*

*Toi* is an indirect object.

Even though *toi* is not, strictly speaking, the beneficiary of the action, it is nevertheless an indirect object. In other words, certain verbs are normally followed by a preposition and the object introduced by that preposition is an indirect object.

---

## H) *Future anterior of conjecture, conditional of unconfirmed information*

The conjecture that requires the use of the future anterior tense is a mental process in which the speaker or writer tries to guess which fact, usually a cause, is the most probable in a series of facts:

*Il est en retard.*
*C'est qu'il aura raté son avion.*

The conditional of unconfirmed information is the result of a simple transmission of information received from another source, without any suppositions and without any judgement, about the probability of the facts. The speaker, or writer in this case, intervenes only to indicate that he/she does not guarantee the accuracy of the information:

*Le tremblement de terre aurait fait des milliers de victimes.*

**Conclusion:** These two operations, one conjecture, the other transmission of information, have nothing in common except that they both refer to facts that are uncertain.

**Note:** i) The future anterior of conjecture most often responds to the question *Why?*

ii) The conditional of unconfirmed information is a construction normally found in the media. When encountered elsewhere, it usually means, *on dit que, on chuchote que*:

*Son goût immodéré pour le risque serait pour quelque chose dans cette faillite.*

**Beware:** Textbooks refer to the conditional of supposition. The above explanation is a demonstration that no such structure exists.

---

*l) Present participle and gerundive*

**The present participle**

The verbal form that ends in the suffix *-ant* is the present participle. It is generally invariable, although, in certain cases, it does vary and is then called the verbal adjective *(adjectif verbal)*. The use and agreement of the latter form is beyond the scope of this study.

The present participle corresponds (as does the verbal adjective) to the form ending in *-ing* of English verbs and is its equivalent in most cases:

*Il portait une lourde valise, changeant de main de temps en temps et s'épongeant le front de son mouchoir.*

The present participle may often be replaced by a relative clause, without changing the meaning:

*Il avait été réveillé de grand matin par sa chienne aboyant contre le laitier (= par sa chienne, qui aboyait contre le laitier).*

## The gerundive

When the participle is preceded by the preposition *en*, it is called the gerundive.

The gerundive is used in four specific instances:

i.  To express the means used:

    They gained access to the vault by digging
    a 15 metre tunnel under the museum.
    *Ils ont pénétré dans la chambre forte **en
    creusant** un tunnel de 15 mètres sous le
    musée.*

ii.  To express manner:

    She welcomed us smiling (or: with a smile).
    *Elle nous a accueillis **en souriant** (ou:
    avec un sourire; ou: avec le sourire).*

iii.  To express cause:

    Louis broke his leg falling from a ladder.
    *Louis s'est cassé la jambe **en tombant**
    d'une échelle.*

iv.  To express concomitance (that is, to indicate that something is happening at the same time as something else).

    Whistle while you work.
    *Siffler **en travaillant**.*

    ***En absorbant** machinalement son petit
    déjeuner, il lisait son journal, qu'il avait
    adossé à la cafetière.*

## The intensified gerundive *(Le gérondif renforcé)*

The gerundive expressing concomitance (*iv* above) is intensified by *tout* when there are two actions that are difficult to perform at the same time or not usually performed at the same time.

In the first expression in example iv, *siffler en travaillant*, it would be absurd to say or write *siffler tout en travaillant* because there is no contradiction between the two actions; on the contrary, they are considered as going very well together and quite normal.

Following are two examples that are self-explanatory and illustrate the use of the intensified gerundive.

    a) *Tout en maintenant le volant aussi fermement qu'elle le pouvait de la main gauche, Ginette s'efforçait de parer de la main droite les coups de langue du labrador, qui s'était apparemment mis en tête de l'aider à conduire la voiture en s'asseyant sur ses genoux.*

    b) *Tout en régalant la compagnie du récit de ses aventures en Extrême-Orient, il ne perdait pas un coup de dent et, sans avoir l'air d'y toucher, faisait un sort au pâté de lièvre de la tante Félicie.*

**Note:** There are cases in which one does not know if there is a possible contradiction between the two simultaneous actions. (Example b could fit into this category). In these cases, the use of *tout* would, of course, depend on the interpretation of the author of the sentence and the nuance he or she wants to express.

## 5) CONJUNCTIONS

---

*Causal conjunctions*

**Parce que** (restrictive or essential clauses)

*Parce que* is the only causal conjunction to answer the question "Why?"

The sentence constructed with *parce que* exists solely to give the reason for something and nothing else:

> *Je ne sors pas parce qu'il pleut.*
> The only reason for the sentence is to tell
> you why I'm not going out.

**Car** (non-restrictive or non-essential clauses)

*Car* adds information to the sentence, but the sentence and the reason for the sentence would not be affected if this part were omitted.

> *Je ne sors pas car il pleut.*
> The fact that it is raining is incidental. The
> purpose of the sentence is to tell you that
> I'm not going out.

## Comme

*Comme* has the same function and meaning as *car* except that it is the first element of the sentence.

> *Comme il pleut, je ne sors pas.*

## Puisque

*Puisque* is used when what is being discussed in the subordinate clause is known in advance.

> *Puisque ma voiture ne roule pas aujour-d'hui, j'aimerais emprunter la vôtre.*

## Vu que, étant donné que

Equivalents sometimes of *comme*, sometimes of *puisque*, rarely of *car*, these expressions are used primarily in legal and administrative French.

**Attendu que** is used only in court judgements.

# 6) ADJECTIVES

## A) The position of the adjective (Part 1)

The position of the adjective depends on

i.  The respective length of the noun and of the adjective: the longer of the two follows, especially if there is a big difference:

> C'est un charmant rhinocéros.
> C'est un chat séduisant.

ii.  The meaning

If it is secondary (i.e., it can be omitted), it precedes the noun:

> J'aimerais bien visiter ce magnifique pays.

If it is fundamental (i.e., it cannot be omitted), it follows the noun:

> Ce sont des souliers à talons hauts.

iii.  Certain fixed usages:

Colours follow the noun.

Certain adjectives precede the noun (see Position of the Adjective, Part 2).

**Note:** Agreement of the adjective when it is a colour: when the colour is indicated by a noun, the noun is invariable (des robes orange, des robes jacynthe, des robes pervenche).

## B) The position of the adjective (Part 2)

The following adjectives normally precede the noun. They are arranged in eclectic pairs that may help you remember them:

gros et *haut*

*vieux* et *nouveau*

*jeune* et *joli*

*grand* ou *petit*

*vilain* ou *beau*

pas *court* mais *long*

si c'est *mauvais* ce n'est pas *bon*

# 7) ARTICLES

## A) Parts of the body

i. When speaking or writing about moving a part of one's own body, French uses the definite article:

*Il leva la tête.*

ii. When one part of the body interacts with another, use *se* (reflexive pronoun) and the definite article:

*Je me lave les mains.*

iii. When one interacts with another person, use the **personal** pronoun and the definite article:

*Elle lui prit la main.*

**Exception:** When the noun is modified, use the possessive adjective *(Elle leva sa jolie tête)* unless *gauche* or *droit* is used *(Il leva le bras droit).*

**Note:** The noun may be modified by an adjective or by a clause (see the following exercise, example b).

  iv. After the verb, use the definite article.

> *Elle a mal à la tête.*
> But
> *Son mal de tête est passé.*
>
> *Il a le front haut, les cheveux noirs.*
> But
> *Son front est haut, ses cheveux sont noirs.*

◻ EXERCISE:

Fill in the blank with the appropriate definite article or possessive adjective.

a. *Il hocha* _____ *tête chauve.*

b. *Il écarta* _____ *pied qu'une chaîne retenait.*

c. *Il tendit* _____ *bras droit.*

KEY:

a.  *sa*

b.  *son*

c.  *le*

## B) Français/le français

In French, names of languages are normally preceded by the definite article.

*J'aime le français.*

Only the verb *parler* is followed by the name of the language without the article.

*Je parle français.*

The article can be used with the verb *parler* to mean *I can speak French* and not *I'm speaking French* (at this moment).

*Je parle le français.*
*J'écris le français.*

*J'écris le français* means *I can write French*, whereas *I'm writing in French* (at this moment) is *J'écris en français.*

*Je parle et j'écris le français* means *I can speak and write French.*

# 8) ADVERBS

## A) Negatives

The French negative is *ne ... pas*, or *ne* completed by one or more of the following: *jamais, personne, rien, plus, aucun*, etc. The omission of *ne* constitutes an error in written French.

*Il ne vient plus jamais personne.*

**Note:** When *ne* is completed by *pas* (or *point*), no additional negative term from the above may be used.

## B) Position of adverbs

i.  What is the usual position of the adverb in a sentence with a simple verb?

> Jean sait **aussi** le français.
> John **also** knows French.

The adverb usually follows a simple verb directly.

ii.  What is the position of most common adverbs in sentences with compound verbs?

> Nous avons **beaucoup** travaillé.
> We worked a great deal.

In sentences with compound tenses, most common adverbs not ending in -ment are placed between the auxiliary verb and the past participle and after pas.

A few adverbs or adverbial expressions of time, such as demain, hier, aujourd'hui, ici and là are normally somewhat stressed and usually come at the end of the sentence:

> Il est revenu hier.

## 9) MISCELLANEOUS

## A) It is, he is (Part 1)

i.  Things

Use il est (elle est) when the verb être is followed by an adjective without a noun.

Use c'est when the verb être is followed by a noun, even if it is accompanied by an adjective.

*Voilà votre chambre.* **Elle** *est très* **claire**.
*C'est* **une belle** *chambre.*

## Exceptions:

a. Use *c'est* when the pronoun is not replacing a specific noun.

   *Vous n'avez pas encore perdu vos lunettes aujourd'hui.* **C'est** *étonnant.*

b. Certain adjectives (*évident, étonnant, facile, difficile, possible, impossible,* etc.) are used with *il est* when followed by *de* or *que* and with *c'est* in other cases:

   *Il est difficile* **de** *sortir d'ici.*
   *Oui,* **c'est** *difficile.*

   *Il est évident* **qu**'il n'a rien compris.*
   *Oui,* **c'est** *évident.*

ii. Something previously mentioned (This is her dog. **It is** a funny animal.)

When **it is** directly refers to something that has been previously mentioned, French uses *il est* or *c'est* depending on the words following **it is**:

a. If **it is** is followed by an adjective without a noun, French uses *il est*:

   This is your room. It is rather small.
   *Voici votre chambre.* **Elle** *est plutôt petite.*

b. If **it is** is followed by a noun (or a pronoun), French uses *c'est*:

   This is your room. It is a small room.
   *Voici votre chambre.* **C'est** *une petite* **chambre**.

iii. Certain adjectives

Certain adjectives may be followed by *de* or *que*, in which case French uses *il est*.

It is difficult to say no.
*Il est difficile de dire non.*

It is obvious that they have left.
*Il est évident qu'ils sont partis.*

When the same adjectives are not followed by *de* or *que*, French uses *c'est*. (General neutral)

It is difficult to say.
*C'est difficile à dire.*

It is obvious.
*C'est évident.*

iv. Here it is: *le voici*. Here she/he is: *La voici. Le voici.*

v. People

To establish personal status (race, nationality, profession, religion, politics ... )

a. In order to indicate someone's identity (answering the question *qui est-ce?*), use *c'est* + article + noun:

*Qui est ce monsieur?*
*C'est un professeur de lycée.*

b. In order to indicate any other idea, use *il est* + noun, without an article:

*Que fait-il dans la vie?*
*Il est professeur de lycée.*

**Nationality:**

*Monsieur Thibaut est français.*
*C'est un Français.*

**Religion:**

*Elle est protestante.*
*C'est une protestante.*

**Political affiliation:**

*Jacques est libéral.*
*C'est un libéral.*

**Official position:**

*Il est ministre.*
*C'est un ministre.*

**Personal status:**

*Il est prisonnier.*
*C'est un prisonnier.*

If the noun is accompanied by an adjective, use *c'est*:

Example:   *Voilà le médecin.*
          There is the doctor.

          *C'est un bon médecin.*
          He is a good doctor.

When personal status is not involved, the rules outlined in part (i) apply.

---

## B)  It is (Part 2)

i. Atmospheric condition

**Rule:** When **it is** is followed by an adjective expressing atmospheric conditions, use *il fait*.

> It is cold.         *Il fait froid.*
>
> It is dark.         *Il fait noir (sombre).*

**Exception:** When the adjective is translated by a noun in French,
**it is** is not translated by *il fait* in today's French, but
by *il y a*.

> It is sunny, the weather is sunny.
> *Il y a du soleil.*

**Note:** This exception is generally unknown in Canada. (*Il fait
soleil, il fait du soleil.*)

  ii. Time

    **It is** expressing time is translated by *il est*.

> It is 8 o'clock.      *Il est huit heures.*
>
> It is late.         *Il est tard.*

  iii. General neutral

    When **it is** is used as a general neutral referring to nothing
specific, it is translated by *c'est*.

> It's wonderful.     *C'est merveilleux.*
> It's beautiful.      *C'est beau.*
> It's all right.      *C'est bon.*
> It's high.         *C'est haut.*

## C) You can see...

The verb *pouvoir* is not normally used with verbs of perception.

You can see ...    *Vous voyez ...*

One could hear ... *On entendait ...*

□ EXERCISE:

Translate the following sentences:

a. Can you smell it?

b. They could hear him screaming.

c. Can you see that tree at the front of the hill?

d. From our hotel room we could hear the sound of the surf.

e. I fail to understand why ...

KEY:

a.  *Tu le sens?*

b.  *Ils l'entendaient crier.*

c.  *Vous voyez cet arbre au pied de la colline?*

d.  *De notre chambre d'hôtel nous entendions le bruit du ressac.*

e.  *Je ne comprends pas pourquoi ...*

## D) Gender

Students lament the fact that it is impossible to know if a noun is masculine or feminine in French, without committing it to memory, and they claim that this difficulty constitutes a serious obstacle to learning the language. While it is true that learning the gender of French nouns is, for the most part, a result of living the language, consider for a moment the problem of the French speaker learning English. Every single time a French speaker pronounces an English word of more than one syllable, he must try to figure out where to put the stress. Is it TRANS por ta tion, trans POR ta tion, or trans por TA tion? French speakers throw up their hands in despair when faced with the following stress pattern: DI plo mat, di PLO macy, di plo MA tic. Needless to say, the English speaker is not presented with any such dilemma when learning French. In French, the last syllable carries the accent tonique.

Pointing this out in no way makes learning French genders easier for the English-speaking student, of course, but it is a sobering thought and puts the matter into perspective. English is easy only if you know it already. The same is true for French. In the meantime, those who want to learn the others' language would do well to prepare themselves to face real difficulties.

---

## E) Negatives and positives: inversion

Sometimes one language will express a certain reality in positive terms, whereas the other will see fit to express the same idea in negative terms. The following are a few examples:

Remember to get ...
*N'oublie pas d'acheter ...*

It's as simple as that.
*Ce n'est pas plus difficile que ça.*

Don't misunderstand me.
*Comprenez-moi bien.*

Shallow
*peu profond*

## F) Guarantee

While it is as foolish to offer a guarantee with a French course as it is with a weight-loss clinic, teachers of French are tempted to offer the following guarantee to students:

Check two aspects of every sentence you write and your marks will increase by 10%:

1. Does every adjective agree with the noun it describes?

2. Does the verb agree with its subject?

This would of course have to be a limited warranty: limited by the linguistic vigilance of the student.

Part Two

# Vocabulary

# 1) TEST

## General

*J'estime qu'il vaut mieux ne pas leur donner leur note sans leur faire subir une épreuve quelconque.* (some kind of test)

cf. *mettre à l'épreuve* (to put to the test)

## School

*Je leur donne une interrogation (écrite)* [colloquially: *une interro*] *tous les quinze jours: un contrôle* is often used.

An oral test or an oral exam is always *un examen oral*.

*Je demanderai au psychotechnicien de faire subir à tous les élèves de seconde un test d'intelligence et un test de mémoire.*

*Que le cours soit semestriel ou annuel, peu importe, il faut leur faire faire un examen tous les semestres.*

## Medical

*Comme le docteur ne trouve pas ce que j'ai, il veut que j'aille au laboratoire pour une série d'analyses.*

A blood test: *une analyse du sang. Un électrocardiogramme est une mesure.*

## Miscellaneous

Driving test: *examen du permis de conduire*

Road test: *essai sur route*

# 2) ÊTRE EN ACCORD OR ÊTRE D'ACCORD?

*être en accord = être en harmonie*

*Nous aimons tous les deux les longues promenades dans les bois; nous sommes en accord sur ce point.* (i.e., our views coincide)

> *être d'accord* = to agree on something (a fact)

> *Denise et moi nous sommes d'accord pour vendre notre maison.* (i.e., we discussed it and we agreed on it)

**Note:** One could say *Nous sommes en accord* or *d'accord sur la façon d'élever nos enfants* depending on whether the points of view happened to coincide or the issue had been discussed and agreed upon.

## 3) RELATIVES

> *Nous avons **de la famille** en Belgique.*

> *Nous logerons chez **des cousins**.*

> *Nous irons voir **les oncles et les tantes** de Robert.*

> *J'ai, moi aussi, **des parents assez éloignés**.*

> *Divers **membres de la famille** se sont occupés de nous.*

In general, **my relatives** can be translated in French by *ma famille. Parents,* in the plural, usually refers to a mother and father in French. You should use the term *famille* as the equivalent of **relatives** or, as indicated in some of the sentences above, be specific and name the relations involved. (Note that in the sentence *Ce sont des parents de ma femme*, the indefinite article would be sufficient to indicate that we are referring to relatives other than mother and father.)

## 4) HOLIDAY, VACATION

i.   *Congé* is a day off or a period of time off.

   *Il est en congé aujourd'hui.*
   He's off today.

   on leave: *être en congé*

   *Un congé sabbatique* is a sabbatical leave.
   To take a leave of absence is *prendre un congé pour convenance personnelle.* (see example iv, below)

ii.  *Vacances* means vacation.

   An institution *(école, parlement, tribunaux)* closes its doors and is *en vacances*:

   *les vacances scolaires*
   *les vacances parlementaires*
   *les vacances judiciaires*

iii. *Fête* is a special day.

   *La Saint-Valentin est une fête.*
   Thanksgiving Day (*La Fête de l'Action de Grâce*)

iv.  *Jour de sortie:*

   *Un domestique a un jour de sortie.* (A day off)

   *Jour de congé:*

   Any other person's day off (e.g., a salesperson)

v.  *Recevoir une permission*: to get a furlough

> *Il est en permission.*
> He is on furlough.

vi.  A *jour férié* is a public holiday.

## 5) DÉCIDER

|  |  |
|---|---|
| To decide to: | *décider de* |
| To decide that: | *décider que* |
| To make up one's mind to: | *se décider à* |
| To be determined to: | *être décidé à* |

> *Elle décida qu'elle devait démissionner.*
> She decided that she must resign.

> *Les ouvriers ont décidé de faire la grève.*
> The workers decided to go on strike.

> *Je ne peux pas me décider à entreprendre cette tâche.*
> I can't make up my mind (bring myself) to undertake this task.

> *Il est décidé à réussir à l'examen.*
> He is determined to pass the exam.

## 6) POUVOIR AND PUISSANCE (POWER)

*Pouvoir* is an action or the result of an action. It is what one is capable of doing or authorised to do. Synonyms are *influence* or *authority*.

> *La politique c'est la recherche du pouvoir.*
> Politics is the quest for power.

*Le pouvoir de cette femme sur son mari est énorme.*

This woman's hold (influence, power) over her husband is enormous.

*Quels sont les pouvoirs du Premier ministre du Canada?*

What powers does the Prime Minister of Canada have?

*Puissance* is an inherent quality. It is what powerful people or institutions possess. Synonyms are force, or intensity and volume (relating to sounds).

*Au conseil de sécurité des Nations Unies les grandes puissances seules ont le droit de véto.*

At the U.N. Security Council only the great powers have the veto.

*La puissance des grosses sociétés industrielles est considérable.*

The power of large corporations is considerable.

*La puissance du moteur d'une voiture s'exprime en chevaux.*

The power of a car's engine is expressed in horsepower.

*N'augmentez pas la puissance du poste, on ne s'entend plus!*

Don't increase the volume, we can't hear ourselves think!

□ EXERCISE:

Fill in the blanks with *puissance* or *pouvoir*.

a. _____ *ne consiste pas à frapper fort ou souvent, mais à frapper juste.* (Balzac)

b. _____ tend à corrompre, et _____ absolu(e) corrompt absolument. (Lord Acton)

c. Tout(e) _____ est faible à moins que d'être uni(e). (La Fontaine)

d. Tout(e) _____ légitime est issu(e) d'une usurpation.

e. L'humilité sert à agir avec _____

f. Tout(e) _____ sans contrôle rend fou.

g. Dans le caractère de notre nation, il y a toujours une tendance à exercer la force, quand on la possède, ou les prétentions du (de la) _____ quand on le tient en main.

h. Il n'y a pas le (la) _____ il y a l'abus de _____ rien d'autre.

KEY:

a.  La puissance

b.  Le pouvoir, le pouvoir

c.  puissance

d.  pouvoir

e.  puissance

f.  pouvoir

g.  pouvoir

h.  pouvoir, pouvoir

# 7) TO SUGGEST

The verb *suggérer* means *advise tactfully and diplomatically*. Synonyms are: *conseiller, proposer, recommander*.

*Je leur ai suggéré d'aller à la plage.*

The verb **to suggest** is expressed by a large number of other verbs in French:

i) His handshake suggested uncommon strength *(une force peu connue)*.
   Here, French would use *dénoter, indiquer* or *révéler*.

ii) He suggested that the doctor might have been delayed by a traffic accident.
   French verbs: *faire remarquer, faire observer*

iii) His grey beard and navy-blue cap suggested deep-sea voyages and South Pacific islands.
   French verbs: *évoquer, faire penser à*

iv) He suggested you were having an affair with his sister.
   French verbs: *insinuer, donner à penser, laisser supposer, prétendre*

# 8) TO VISIT

To visit a city or a place (e.g., a museum) is usually *aller* or *venir*:

He visited Waterloo on Sunday.
*Il est venu dimanche à Waterloo.*

I'll visit the British Museum.
*J'irai au British Museum.*

To pay a visit to a person is *aller voir* or *rendre visite à*:

She visited her aunt.
*Elle est allée voir sa tante.*

OR

*Elle a rendu visite à sa tante.*

**Note:** *Visiter* is used to express visit when a close examination is understood:

*Le médecin visite son malade.*
*Le touriste visite une ville.*

## 9) SE SERVIR DE

*Se servir de* is normally used in the following cases:

i)   as the means to perform a given act:

*On s'est servi d'une poutre pour enfoncer la porte.*

ii)  to turn something to (good) account *(mettre à profit)*:

*Son père lui a appris à se servir de ses poings.*

iii) to exploit someone:

*Ne voyez-vous pas qu'il se sert de vous?*

## 10) SCARCELY, HARDLY

When scarcely or hardly means no sooner, it is translated *à peine (than* would be *que).*

**Note:** *A peine* begins the sentence or clause and the verb is inverted.

> *A peine étions-nous entrés qu'un incident éclata.*

## 11) COULD, WOULD

These words normally require either the imperfect or conditional tense in French, depending on the context.

> I couldn't come yesterday.
>
> As a boy, I would go to chapel every day.

The above sentences require the imperfect tense in French.

> We could leave tomorrow, if you agree.
>
> They would have fought with their bare hands, if need be.

The above sentences require the conditional (or conditional perfect) tense in French.

To determine the tense required, you must ask yourself: "Has the action been performed or not?"

i. Would

   a. If the action has been performed, it may represent

   1. A wish in the past:

   He wouldn't do it. (i.e., He refused to do it.)
   *Il ne voulait pas le faire.*
   (possibly: *Il n'a pas voulu le faire.*)

   2. A habit or custom in the past:

   She would walk her dog twice a day.

*Elle promenait son chien deux fois par jour.*

b. When the action has not been performed, the conditional is used:

I would like to go there.
*J'aimerais y aller.*

I would do it if I had the time.
*Je le ferais si j'avais le temps.*

I would have done it if I had had the time.
*Je l'aurais fait si j'avais eu le temps.*

ii. Could

a. If the action has been performed, it may represent a possibility in the past:

I couldn't do it.
*Je ne pouvais pas le faire.*
(possibly: *Je n'ai pas pu le faire.*)

I could have taken it yesterday.
*J'aurais pu le prendre hier.*

b. When the action has not been performed, the conditional is used:

I could go myself, if I had the money.
*Je pourrais y aller moi-même, si j'avais l'argent.*

**Summary:** To translate the English words **could** and **would**, use the French imperfect (or *passé simple/composé*) when the action has been performed, and the French conditional (*conditional anterior*) when the action has not been performed.

## 12) OUI OR SI?

**Yes** is translated by *si* in French

i.   when it is an affirmative answer to a negative question:

*N'as-tu pas faim?*
*- Si!*

ii.  when it contradicts a negative statement:

*Ce n'est pas moi!*
*- Si, c'est toi!*

## 13) D'AVANCE/À L'AVANCE

*On sait **d'avance** ce qu'on va se dire.*

*J'étais maintenant résigné **d'avance** à tout.*

*Tout a été préparé **à l'avance**.*

*Une heure **à l'avance**.*

*D'avance* (used after a verb) and *à l'avance* are synonyms and mean *in advance, beforehand.*

*Il est en avance d'une heure. (opposite of late)*

*En avance* means *ahead of* time, *before* time, *early.*

## 14) MENER/PORTER

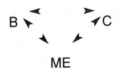

i.  From B to C or from C to B:

> *mener/porter*

a.  *Elle **mène** son mari par le bout du nez.*

b.  *On peut **mener** un cheval à l'abreuvoir, mais on ne peut pas le forcer à boire.*

c.  *Le petit Chaperon Rouge **portait** une galette et un pot de beurre à sa grand'mère.*

In (a) and (b) someone is leading someone or something; in (c) someone is carrying something.

ii.  From B to Me:

a)  *Amener/apporter*

> *Amène ta soeur et apporte quelques disques de danse.*

b)  *Ramener/rapporter* express two possibilities:

1.  a person or a thing is or will be returned to me

> My Bonnie lies over the ocean
> My Bonnie lies over the sea
> Bring back my Bonnie to me ...

> ***Ramenez**-moi ma Bonnie.*

2.  ***Rapporte**-moi mon livre dès que tu l'auras lu.*

3.  A person or a thing comes to me for the first time, but through an intermediary who is returning.

> *Quand il est revenu de chez la tante Ursule, il a **ramené** un Saint-Bernard*

*aussi grand qu'un veau.*

*Elle m'a **rapporté** de son voyage au Mexique trois ceintures en cuir repoussé.*

iii. From Me to B:

Either *mener/porter* or *emmener/emporter* is used, depending on the circumstances.

a. *Mener/porter* are used when the move of a person or a thing, represented by the direct object, is the main reason for the action.

1. *As-tu **porté** la poubelle dans la rue?*

   *Tous les jours je dois **mener** les enfants à l'école.*

2. *Emmener* (take along ... a person)/*emporter* (take along = carry) are used when the move of the person or thing represented by the direct object is not the main purpose of the action:

   *Nous **emporterons** des sandwichs au lieu d'aller manger au restaurant.*

   (We'll take them with us, but our main purpose is to go somewhere to do something, not to take sandwiches.)

3. *Emmener/emporter* are also used when the meaning is to take away.

   *Débarrassez-moi de ce casse-pied.*

   ***Emmenez-le** où vous voulez, pourvu que je ne le voie plus.*

□ EXERCISE:

Fill in the blank with the correct form of the appropriate verb:

a. *La mère* _____ *son enfant dans ses bras.*

b. *Le vieux colonel* _____ *ses troupes au feu.*

c. *On nous* _____ *les enfants tous les matins.*

d. *Je vais te* _____ *en voiture.*

e. *Le vent d'ouest nous* _____ *toutes les fumées d'usine.*

f. *N'oublie pas de lui* _____ *son para-pluie.*

g. *Nous* _____ *des vêtements chauds.*

KEY:

| | | |
|---|---|---|
| a. *porte* | b. *menait* | c. *amène* |
| d. *ramener* | e. *apporte* | f. *rapporter* |
| g. *emportons (portons)* | | |

## 15) SANS DOUTE AND OTHER FALSE FRIENDS

*Sans doute* means *probably.* If you want to say *doubtless* or *without doubt* you must say *sans aucun doute.*

There are other *faux amis* that are not as well known as the obvious ones, such as *librairie.*

*Éventuellement* does not mean eventually, but rather *possibly.*

*Actuellement* does not mean actually, but

rather *currently*.

*Séculaire* does not mean secular but rather *age-old*.

## 16) S'ASSURER QUE

*S'assurer que* has two similar, but not identical, meanings:

i. *Veiller à ce que, faire en sorte que* **followed by the subjunctive** (verbs of volition)

*Assurez-vous que cet homme éminent soit traité avec les égards qui lui sont dus.*

ii. *Vérifier si* (to check) **followed by the indicative** (verbs of opinion, perception, etc.)

*Je me suis assuré avant de partir que toutes les portes étaient verrouillées.*

## 17) FOOD ... FOR THOUGHT

*Nourriture* is the general term that represents all of the substances that living beings consume to assure their survival.

*Trouver sa **nourriture** c'est facile, dit le poulet; mais trouver un coin où la manger en paix, c'est autre chose.*

(Proverbe bantou)

It is also the word used to convey a figurative meaning:

*La "télé" quotidienne lui fournit, semble-t-il, toute la **nourriture** spirituelle dont il a besoin.*

However, the term *aliment* is used in certain cases with a figurative meaning:

*Au détriment de sa santé il s'obstinait à se passionner sans réserve pour tout ce qui apportait des **aliments** à son courroux.*

But, in its normal usage, *aliment* denotes one of the substances that a person or an animal eats.

*Il faudrait limiter votre consommation **d'aliments** contenant une proportion considérable de graisse.*

*Il écrasait et mélangeait ses **aliments** dans son assiette au point de les réduire en une bouillie informe.*

When the word **food** is used in business or agriculture, it is referred to as *denrées alimentaires*.

*Ils produisent bien quelques **denrées alimentaires** pour leur propre subsistance, mais ils n'en exportent pas.*

*Il semble bien qu'en Amérique du Nord les **denrées alimentaires** n'aient pas automatiquement leur place dans les magasins à rayons multiples.*

When **food** is considered gastronomically, it is *cuisine* or more elegantly *la table*.

In more popular usage, it is said that *on mange bien* whereas *on fait bonne chère*, or one even refers to *la chère* in literary and mannered French.

*La **cuisine** belge traditionnelle et bourgeoise est encore plus riche que la **cuisine** française.*

*L'hôtel ne date pas d'hier: le décor est vieillot et les robinets font beaucoup de bruit; mais **la table** est de tout premier ordre.*

*Nous avons passé les vacances de Noël dans une petite station alpestre peu con-*

*nue: on n'y faisait pas beaucoup de ski, mais on **y mangeait bien.***

*Victor Hugo, Alexandre Dumas, Balzac étaient des hommes corpulents. On dirait qu'il y a, chez les écrivains prolifiques, une tendance commune à **faire bonne chère.***

*Je ne pardonne pas à la Marquise le tour pendable qu'elle m'a joué: j'avais comme voisin de table le vicomte d'Argentcourt, qui m'a rasée jusqu'à l'os. Mais il faut concéder que, en compensation, **la chère** était délectable.*

Dogs and cats eat their *pâtée*. Feeding time at the zoo is rendered by *le repas des fauves*. In addition, the verbal form is often used.

*Qui s'occupera des poissons pendant ton absence? Il faudrait tout au moins que quelqu'un se charge de les **nourrir.***

*Si tu es bien sage et si tu ne fatigues pas bobonne, tu pourras **donner à manger** aux poissons.*

**Note:** **Les vivres** are provisions or the food supply.

*Au bout de six semaines, **les vivres** vinrent à manquer.*

**Note:** **Food** can be *mets*: e.g., Chinese food is *mets chinois*. I don't like spicy food is *Je n'aime pas les mets épicés.*

In conclusion, there are at least four French terms that one must keep in mind when rendering the English word *food*: nourriture, aliments, denrées alimentaires and cuisine.

## 18) TRANCHÉ

*Tranché* means *cut off*. One of the articles of the French Constitution used to allow for the following penalty: *Tout condamné à mort aura la tête tranchée*. (In other words, his head will be cut off).

One sees *jambon tranché* and *pain tranché* on packages, which is clearly wrong. The labels should read *jambon (coupé) en tranches* and *pain (coupé) en tranches*.

## 19) EACH/EVERY

i.  *Chaque* means *each* as defined by the Collins English Dictionary: "every (one) of two or more considered individually." There is a group, and each one of the group can be seen separately.

**Example:** Each gave according to his ability. There is a group, but the emphasis is on the individuals that constitute the group.

*A chaque jour suffit sa peine.*

*Une place pour chaque chose et chaque chose à sa place.*

ii.  *Tout (tous, toute, toutes)* means *every* as defined by Collins: "each one (of the class specified), without exception."

Every child knows it.

*Tous les magasins de la ville* (every shop in town) *de tous les pays* (from every country).

*Tous les moyens sont bons.*

**Note:** When either (i) or (ii) applies; that is, when what is referred to can be seen as a single unit individually within a group (i), or as every single unit of the group, without exception (ii), then French allows the use of either *chaque* or *tout*:

> Every movement is painful to him.
> *Chaque mouvement* or *Tout mouvement lui fait mal.*

> Each isolated movement hurts him, and every movement without exception hurts him.

at every moment:

> *à tout moment* or *à chaque instant*, depending on the emphasis: every single moment or each isolated moment.

Why would one almost certainly not write this?:

> *Chaque jour elle travaille à la bibliothèque pendant trois heures.*

**Answer:** If the writer means that she works at the library for three hours every day without exception, he should have written:

> *Elle travaille tous les jours à la bibliothèque pendant trois heures.*

## 20) ENCORE AND TOUJOURS

*Toujours* is used in place of *encore* to intensify or reinforce the meaning, suggesting that the limits of a reasonable period of time have been exceeded:

i.  *Je sais que vous avez rendez-vous à 9 heures chez le dentiste. J'ai moi-même rendez-vous à 9 heures et demie chez ce dentiste, mais avec son hygiéniste. En arrivant à 9 heures et demie, je vous trouve là, piaffant, dans la salle d'attente.*

- *"Oh! Vous êtes **encore** là!"*

*Et quand je sors une heure plus tard, je vous retrouve, exaspéré et vous rongeant les poings, dans la salle d'attente, je m'exclame:*

- *"Comment? Vous êtes **toujours** là!"*

ii. Le fils de ma voisine a terminé ses études il y a deux ans et il est **toujours** sans travail.

## 21) WHEN IS A *RUE* NOT A STREET?

It would never occur to any French-speaking writer or journalist to write: *Sa fille avait épousé un célèbre médecin de la rue Harley* or *Il avait rêvé à vingt ans de devenir un grand financier de la rue Wall.* Harley Street, Wall Street, Downing Street, the *Königstrasse* and the *Puerta del Sol* are invariable names that are used such as they are in any language without being altered.

Applying the same principle and usage, one can see that there is no *rue Yonge* in Toronto — it's Yonge Street whether you're speaking French or English. For a *rue Yonge* to exist, Toronto would have to be a French city, or at least a bilingual one, in which case the street signs would reflect the French usage.

However, even if the city were French or bilingual, there wouldn't be a *rue Church* in Toronto, because Church Street would be *rue de l'Église* in French. Neither would there be a *rue Collège*, because College Street would be translated as *rue du Collège*.

Here is the rule: In the names of streets, the word *rue* is followed by the preposition *de* (or by *du* or *des*) unless a proper name is involved.

**Note:** This rule applies equally to avenue, place, etc.

*Avenue de l'Université*

*Avenue des Champs Elysées*

*Avenue des Nations*

*Avenue du Général de Gaulle*

*Place de la Concorde*

*Rue des Cordeliers*

*Boulevard de la Reine*

*Avenue Marie-Thérèse*

*Avenue Winston Churchill*

It is perhaps worth mentioning that, in Old French, major thoroughfares were *chemins*. (Hence the term *voleur de grand chemin* — highwayman). However, today *chemins* are small, country roads. One speaks now of *grand-routes*, or *grandes routes*, rather than *grands chemins*. In modern French, the equivalent of road is *route*, and so Westmount Road, for example, is *Route de Westmount*, and not *Chemin Westmount* as it is often mistakenly called.

The same is true of peoples' names. *Pierre Dubé* is not Peter Dubé in English. It's *Pierre Dubé* in any language.

## 22) ESPOIR/ESPÉRANCE

In modern French, **hope** is normally expressed as *espoir*:

*Dans l'espoir d'un accueil favorable à ma requête, je vous prie d'agréer ...*

*Seul l'espoir du retour de Jean-Luc lui permettrait de continuer.*

*Espérance* is, for the most part, a literary or religious term:

*Mon coeur, lassé de tout, même de l'espérance*

*N'ira plus de ses voeux importuner le sort.*

(Lamartine)

61

> *Abandonnez toute espérance, vous qui entrez.* (Dante)

*Espérance* is reserved, as well, for special uses and expressions:

> *Il a de belles espérances du côté de son oncle.* (an inheritance)
>
> *Cet étudiant donne de grandes espérances.* (shows a lot of promise)
>
> *Foi, espérance et charité* (Faith, hope and charity)
>
> *Espérance de vie* (life expectancy: neologism based on English)

## 23) NUMBERS, FIGURES AND DIGITS

The English word *figure* poses no problem. The French equivalent of this mathematical term is *chiffre*.

The English word *digit* has no French equivalent. No French word means both *lettre* and *chiffre*.

One gets around the problem by the use of two words:

> *Dans notre pays, les plaques d'immatriculation des véhicules à moteur comportent normalement six lettres ou chiffres* (six digits).

The English word *number* can be either *nombre* or *numéro* depending on the meaning.

*Nombre* tells you how many units there are of a given kind:

> *Il a la passion des chapeaux: il possède un nombre incroyable de couvre-chefs de toutes formes et de toutes couleurs.*
>
> *Pour répartir les locaux il faudrait connaître*

*le nombre d'étudiants qu'il y a dans chaque classe.*

*Nous avons besoin d'un grand nombre de tracteurs.*

*Numéro* tells you the **position** a given unit occupies in a series.

*Numéro* often (see examples 2, 3, 4) serves to **identify** a unit, i.e., to distinguish it from other units in the same series.

1. *Veuillez excuser mon retard: j'avais le numéro 12 au comptoir des charcuteries.*

2. *Nous sommes presque voisins: il habite au numéro 27, moi au 22.*

3. *Je n'ai jamais gagné à la loterie: je collectionne les mauvais numéros.*

4. *Je vais vous donner mon numéro de téléphone.*

**Note:** There are all kinds of interesting peculiarities:

*Le chiffre de la population d'un pays représente le nombre de ses habitants.*

When one says *Il porte une bague gravée à son chiffre*, the *chiffre* is, in fact, a letter or a series of letters.

One uses *chiffres* to write *nombres* as, for example, in mathematics: *nombres entiers, nombres fractionnaires, nombres décimaux, nombres pairs, nombres impairs, nombres premiers, nombres imaginaires ...*

A circus number is *un numéro de cirque.*

This week's number or issue of a magazine is *le numéro.*

*Un drôle de numéro* is a peculiar character.

**A final note:** The figure most of us struggle to keep by following a strict diet is *la ligne* and the diet is *un régime*.

## 24) THERE ARE WORDS ... AND THERE ARE WORDS: *MOTS/PAROLES*

i.   *Mots* are individual grammatical or lexical units. They are concrete and specific. You can count them. They are something you find in the dictionary. In written form, they are a series of letters; in spoken form, they are a series of sounds:

> *Les télégrammes coûtent 54 cents par mot.*
>
> *Nous pouvons mettre sur votre T-Shirt une inscription de cinq mots maximum.*
>
> *J'aimerais exprimer la même idée à l'aide d'un mot plus élégant.*
>
> *Jean trouve toujours le mot juste pour consoler ses amis.*

ii.  *Paroles* represent an aggregate, words taken as a whole. Spoken at some point, they represent the expression of one or several ideas in written or oral form. The meaning, the message, is the important element:

> *On entend à peine leurs paroles.*
>
> *Il nous a payés de belles paroles.*

**Note**:   In certain cases, writers use *mots* instead of *paroles* for literary or stylistic purposes.

**Note**:   There are many special usages for *mots* and *paroles*.

*Les gros mots* (swear words)

*Glisser un mot* (to put in a word on behalf of someone)

*Avoir des mots avec quelqu'un* (to have words with someone)

*La parole* is the faculty of speech *(J'en perds la parole, je lui passe la parole, couper la parole à quelqu'un).*

*Paroles* are lyrics of a song

*En parole et en fait* (words as opposed to acts)

*Je te donne ma parole* (I give you my word).

□ EXERCISE:

Try your hand at the following:

a. *Ce sont ses propres* _____ (1), *c'est ce qu'il a dit* _____ (2) *pour* _____ (3).

b. *Je ne trouve pas les* _____ (4) *pour exprimer ce que je pense.*

c. *Il nous a tout raconté dans un déluge de* _____ (5).

KEY:

1. *paroles*: an aggregate, words taken as a whole, the expression of an idea.

2. *mot*: a single word.

3. *mot*: a single word.

4. *mots*: the concrete, specific form.

5. *paroles*: an aggregate, words taken as a whole, the expression of an idea.

## 25)  So

English speakers are equipped with a light that goes on when the word *so* is used, and they automatically translate it as *donc*. More thought should be given to the translation of this two-letter word.

In the sentence *We were both too tired to cook, so we had dinner in a restaurant*, the first idea (too tired) is the cause of the second (restaurant); or, if you prefer, the second is the consequence of the first. Translating this as *donc nous sommes allés dîner au restaurant* would not be correct.

A French speaker would say *alors nous sommes allés dîner au restaurant*. A more formal way of expressing this would be *de sorte que nous sommes allés dîner au restaurant*.

The use of *donc* would be acceptable only if it were used after the verb: ... *nous sommes donc allés dîner au restaurant*.

**Note:** He never understands, unless you tell him three times, he's so stupid *(tant il est bête)*.

## 26)  DIMINUTIVES

There are three uses of the diminutive form:

i.   To designate an object of smaller proportions: e.g., *une maisonnette*. The suffix *-et(te)* is a diminutive suffix. The noun *maisonnette* is a diminutive of *maison*.

ii.  To designate the affectionate form of a name (pet name):

E.g., *Louison, Louisette*. The word *Louison* is not shorter than *Louise*, and the person is not shorter than Louise but is rather a diminutive form of the name.

iii. Rare: To designate the shortened form of a word that is not an abbreviation but a shortened form in the vernacular; e.g., *la fac* for *la faculté* and *une interro* for *une interrogation écrite*.

**Note:** This form is more commonly called forme *écourtée,* forme *tronquée* or forme *abrégée.*

## 27) BOUCHÉES, FOURNÉES, SOIRÉES ... CHAQUE JOUR ET CHAQUE ANNÉE: REFLECTIONS ON A SUFFIX

i. General remarks on the suffix *-ée*

The suffix *-ée* normally indicates the contents (le contenu: what something contains) or the capacity (la contenance: the quantity a thing can hold). It usually corresponds to the English suffix *-ful.*

| A mouthful | *une bouchée* |
| *cuillère* | *cuillerée* |
| *gorge* | *gorgée* |
| *charrette* | *charretée* |
| *bras* | *brassée* |
| *four* | *fournée* |

The addition of the suffix *-ée* results in feminine nouns.

**Note:** a. Formation of words containing the suffix is not always obvious:

For *cuillère*, add the suffix;

For *gorgée*, the final *-e* of *gorge* is omitted;

For *charretée*, the final *-e* and one of the *t*'s of *charrette* are omitted;

For *brassée*, the *-s* of *bras* is doubled;

For *fournée*, an *-n* is added to four.

b. The suffix cannot be added indiscriminately; e.g., *une tassée* does not exist. French has no special word to indicate the contents of a cup.

c. Conversely, the word *coupée* (gangway) exists but it is not the contents of *une coupe* (dish, goblet).

d. The word *couvée* (clutch of eggs, brood of chickens) comes from the verb *couver* (to sit on eggs) and not from the non-existent noun *une couve*.

e. Some of the nouns can be used figuratively. The noun *fournée*, for example, like its English equivalent *batch*, is used in the literal sense (contents of a *four*), or in a figurative sense:

> Grâce à la souplesse du système des crédits, l'université peut, en pratique, sortir trois fournées de diplômes chaque année.

In the case of *fournée*, the figurative meaning is slightly pejorative.

ii. *An/année, jour/journée, matin/matinée, soir/soirée*

The use of one or other of these words (e.g., *an* vs *année*) is not the choice between words of equal value. The use of *an*, as opposed to *année*, or *jour* rather than *journée*, for example, is not immaterial. The choice is closely tied to the context and, in most cases, one cannot be substituted for the other.

Some rules are valid for the four pairs of words. We shall begin with those, and then indicate specific rules that govern the use of individual pairs.

a. For all four pairs, the *-ée* form is used:

1. When the noun is accompanied by the adjective *tout(e)* in the feminine singular.

   *Toute l'année*

   *Toute la matinée*

2. When the noun is accompanied by a qualifying adjective.

   *Trois ans/Trois longues années*
   *Un jour d'été/Une belle journée d'été*
   *Un matin/Une matinée bien employée*
   *Un soir de printemps/Une inoubliable soirée de printemps*

3. When a number is accompanied by a relative clause.

   *Les quatre années que j'ai passées en Europe.*
   *C'est une journée qui m'a paru bien longue!*
   *Une de ces matinées dont les préparatifs prennent beaucoup de temps.*
   *Voilà une soirée dont je me souviendrai!*

**Note:** This rule (a. 1, 2 and 3) has precedence over all the following.

b. For all four pairs, the shorter form is used when the noun is accompanied by the adjective *tous* (in the masculine plural) followed by *les*.

   *Tous les ans* (**But**: *toutes ces années*)
   *Tous les jours* (**But**: *toutes nos journées*)

iii. *An/année*

a.  Besides the case mentioned in ii. b, *an* is used after the preposition *par* and after a number.

> *Tous les ans*
>
> *Trois fois par an*
>
> *Un, deux, trois, etc. ... an(s)*

We can conclude, therefore, that one says *tous les ans* (ii, b) but *toutes ces années laborieuses* (ii, a, 2) and *toute l'année* (ii, a, 1).

*An* tends to be used with precise numbers (*un an, treize ans, tous les ans*) and *année* with unspecified numbers *(quelques années, plusieurs années)*. This is not true for the other pairs.

**Note:** One says *cinq ans, neuf ans ...*, but *la 5e année, la 9e année*.

b.  When the subject is the year gone by or the next one, or New Year's Day (Jour de l'An, never Jour de l'Année) accompanied by the adjective nouvel (or neuf), sometimes *an* is used, sometimes *années*, under similar circumstances when the meaning is the same:

> *L'an dernier* or *l'année dernière*
>
> *L'an passé* or *l'année passée*
>
> *L'an prochain* or *l'année prochaine*
>
> *Le Nouvel An* or *La Nouvelle Année*
>
> *L'An neuf* or *l'Année Nouvelle*

**Note:** *L'an dernier, l'année dernière* mean *last year*, but *la dernière année* (a, 2) means *the last year*. Similarly, *l'an prochain, l'année prochaine* mean *next year* but *the next year* is *l'année suivante* (a, 2).

c.  Aside from the cases mentioned in (ii, a), *année*

rather than *an* is used when the noun is accompanied by a noun object (*complément du nom or complément déterminatif*).

*C'était l'année de l'incendie de San Francisco*

**Note:** This rule holds for *an/année* but not for *jour*.

*Ça s'est passé le jour de son anniversaire.*

d. Canadian French differs somewhat: *année* is sometimes used instead of *an* after a number (*six années* rather than *six ans*, etc.)

iv. *Jour/journée*

Other than the case mentioned in (ii, b), *jour* is used in the same way as *an* (see iii, a):

*Tous les jours (ii, b)*
*Trois fois par jour*
*Un, deux, trois, etc. ... jours(s)*

but it is used, in addition, in the following cases:

after an ordinal number:

*Le premier, le deuxième (second), le troisième ... le dernier jour.* (**But**: *la première ... la dernière année.*)

after *ce*:

*ce jour-là* (**But**: *cette année-là*)

after *chaque*:

chaque jour (**But**: *chaque année*)

after a word indicating an unspecified number:

Quelques jours (**But**: *quelques années*)
Plusieurs jours (**But**: *plusieurs années*)

**Summary:**
1. *Tous les jours*
2. *Trois fois par jour*
3. *Quatre jours*
4. *Le cinquième jour, le dernier jour*
5. *Ce jour-là*
6. *Chaque jour*
7. *Quelques jours, plusieurs jours*

In all other cases, the feminine form *journée* is used.

v. *Matin/matinée, soir/soirée*

  a. In addition to the case noted in (ii, b), *matin* and *soir* are used after *ce* and *chaque*:

Tous les matins, tous les soirs (ii, b)
Ce matin, ce soir
Chaque matin, chaque soir

  b. Either form can be used after an ordinal number and after *dernier* but the -ée form is more common.

Comme le premier homme à son premier matin ...
Le troisième soir il s'endormit et ne s'éveilla plus.

*C'était la dernière soirée que nous passions ensemble.*

*La quatrième matinée est occupée par de fastidieux exercices de laboratoire.*

c. In all other cases, the *-ée* form is normally used:

*Toute la soirée*

*Une belle matinée*

*Six soirées par mois*

*Quelques matinées*

*Plusieurs soirées*

*Toutes ces matinées*

*Toutes ces soirées*

vi. Some further thoughts:

As complicated as the above may seem, it merely scratches the surface of the problem. Exceptions have been dropped, nuances omitted. We present here only the basics. To demonstrate this point, consider the following example: in iii b, we presented four terms as synonyms — *l'an dernier, l'année dernière, l'an passé* and *l'année passée*. One cannot, however, substitute one for another, in all cases, at will. The following illustrates the point:

*L'année passée* is the most common form.

*L'année dernière* is one step up the cultural ladder but it is not pretentious.

*L'an dernier* is not affected, but it is careful or studied usage.

*L'an passé* is used, but is literary rather than colloquial.

In much the same way, *le Nouvel An* and *la Nouvelle Année* are used more or less similarly; *l'Année Nouvelle* is more formal, but *l'An neuf* is rather stilted. As we can see then, they are not exact equivalents.

The rules of usage discussed in this modest study of the -ée form are, therefore, neither complete nor highly nuanced. However, if the rules are applied, the user will be correct 90 percent of the time. Not perfect, but not bad either.

## 28. AN EMPLOYEE ISN'T UN EMPLOYÉ

**Note:** Although José Binamé and I spoke in French about all of these points, I wrote the work in English. However, José himself wrote this entry in a note to me and I wanted to preserve it and publish it as he wrote it, not only as a kind of tribute to him, but as an example of his expressive power and style in French. (Paul Socken)

*En principe, un employé travaille dans un bureau (Il y a des variantes comme toujours). Quiconque se livre à un travail manuel pour compte d'un employeur est un ouvrier. Entre les deux il existe une série d'activités qui ne se classent dans aucune de ces catégories tout en donnant lieu à un emploi rétribué plus ou moins régulier, mais nous ne nous proposons pas de nous intéresser à elles pour l'instant.*

*Si la presse française imprime que les employés des usines Renault à Boulogne-Billancourt se sont mis en grève, cela veut dire que les gens qui travaillent derrière un pupitre ou devant un ordinateur dans les bureaux de cette société à cet endroit ont cessé de travailler, mais que les ouvriers des ateliers et des lignes d'assemblage poursuivent la production. Et si l'on veut indiquer que tout le monde en dehors des échelons de direction se croise les bras, on annoncera que le personnel est en grève.*

*Ainsi il ne nous reste qu'un petit problème de langue à résoudre: si on fait allusion en anglais à un seul "employee," quel est l'équivalent français de ce terme? Il n'y en a pas à proprement parler et il faut avoir recours à une périphrase: nous utiliserons ici l'expression "un membre du personnel."*

*Dans les secteurs linguistiques frontaliers anglais-français — c'est le cas du Canada tout entier — il est bon d'attirer l'attention des rédacteurs sur cette petite difficulté de traduction, car les dépêches émanant des agences de presse sont le plus souvent libellées en anglais et la tentation est forte, pour des journalistes pressés, de faire hâtivement appel à des calques de l'anglais, au risque d'être mal compris par les quelque cent millions de francophones qui, dans le domaine des structures fondamentales tout au moins, échappent aux séductions corruptrices de ce voisinage.*

*Résumé: Les employés sont les "white collar workers." Les ouvriers sont les "blue collar workers." Le personnel, ce sont tous les "employees." Un membre du personnel, c'est "an employee."*

## CONCLUSION

Language is as complex as human nature and its limitless expression reflects the culture that gave birth to it. No single book on grammar can explain it; no comments on some of its quirks and idiosyncrasies can do more than illuminate a few corners.

It is the purpose of instructors of a second or foreign language to teach the basics, but also to inspire students to seek what is unique in each language and to reflect on the relationship and interplay between languages. It is during that process that one discovers that one is undertaking a journey called education.